Quilting
project planner

Index

Name	For	Projet no

Index

Name	For	Projet no

Index

Name	For	Projet no

Project no:

Name:_____

For:_____

Date started: _____ Date finished : _____

Pattern: _____

Fabric:_____
Color:_____
Purchased from:_____
Cost: _____

Fabric:_____
Color:_____
Purchased from:_____
Cost: _____

Fabric:_____
Color:_____
Purchased from:_____
Cost: _____

Progress Checklist:

☐ Fabric pulled   ☐ Backing made
☐ Fabric cut   ☐ Quilt basted
☐ Blocks made   ☐ Quilting done
☐ Rows sewn   ☐ Binding made
☐ Borders on   ☐ Binding on

Notes:_____
_____
_____
_____
_____
_____
_____

Design

Picture

Project no:

Name:_____

For:_____

Date started: _____ Date finished : _____

Pattern:_____

Fabric:_____

Color:_____

Purchased from:_____

Cost: _____

Fabric:_____

Color:_____

Purchased from:_____

Cost: _____

Fabric:_____

Color:_____

Purchased from:_____

Cost: _____

Progress Checklist:

☐ Fabric pulled   ☐ Backing made

☐ Fabric cut   ☐ Quilt basted

☐ Blocks made   ☐ Quilting done

☐ Rows sewn   ☐ Binding made

☐ Borders on   ☐ Binding on

Notes:_____

_____

_____

_____

_____

_____

Design

Picture

Project no:

Name:_____

For:_____

Date started: _____ Date finished : _____

Pattern:_____

Fabric:_____

Color:_____

Purchased from:_____

Cost:_____

Fabric:_____

Color:_____

Purchased from:_____

Cost:_____

Fabric:_____

Color:_____

Purchased from:_____

Cost:_____

Progress Checklist:

☐ Fabric pulled   ☐ Backing made

☐ Fabric cut   ☐ Quilt basted

☐ Blocks made   ☐ Quilting done

☐ Rows sewn   ☐ Binding made

☐ Borders on   ☐ Binding on

Notes:_____

_____

_____

_____

_____

_____

Design

Picture

Project no:

Name:_____

For:_____

Date started: _____ Date finished : _____

Pattern: _____

Fabric:_____

Color:_____

Purchased from:_____

Cost:_____

Fabric:_____

Color:_____

Purchased from:_____

Cost:_____

Fabric:_____

Color:_____

Purchased from:_____

Cost:_____

Progress Checklist:

☐ Fabric pulled   ☐ Backing made

☐ Fabric cut   ☐ Quilt basted

☐ Blocks made   ☐ Quilting done

☐ Rows sewn   ☐ Binding made

☐ Borders on   ☐ Binding on

Notes:_____

_____

_____

_____

_____

_____

_____

Design

Picture

Project no:

Name:_____

For:_____

Date started: _____ Date finished : _____

Pattern: _____

Fabric:_____
Color:_____
Purchased from:_____
Cost: _____

Fabric:_____
Color:_____
Purchased from:_____
Cost: _____

Fabric:_____
Color:_____
Purchased from:_____
Cost: _____

Progress Checklist:

☐ Fabric pulled   ☐ Backing made
☐ Fabric cut   ☐ Quilt basted
☐ Blocks made   ☐ Quilting done
☐ Rows sewn   ☐ Binding made
☐ Borders on   ☐ Binding on

Notes:_____
_____
_____
_____
_____
_____

Design

Picture

Project no:

Name: _____

For: _____

Date started: _____ **Date finished :** _____

Pattern: _____

Fabric: _____

Color: _____

Purchased from: _____

Cost: _____

Fabric: _____

Color: _____

Purchased from: _____

Cost: _____

Fabric: _____

Color: _____

Purchased from: _____

Cost: _____

Progress Checklist:

☐ Fabric pulled   ☐ Backing made

☐ Fabric cut   ☐ Quilt basted

☐ Blocks made   ☐ Quilting done

☐ Rows sewn   ☐ Binding made

☐ Borders on   ☐ Binding on

Notes: _____

_____

_____

_____

_____

_____

Design

Picture

Project no:

Name:_____

For:_____

Date started: _____ **Date finished :** _____

Pattern: _____

Fabric:_____

Color:_____

Purchased from:_____

Cost:_____

Fabric:_____

Color:_____

Purchased from:_____

Cost:_____

Fabric:_____

Color:_____

Purchased from:_____

Cost:_____

Progress Checklist:

☐ Fabric pulled ☐ Backing made

☐ Fabric cut ☐ Quilt basted

☐ Blocks made ☐ Quilting done

☐ Rows sewn ☐ Binding made

☐ Borders on ☐ Binding on

Notes:_____

_____

_____

_____

_____

_____

Design

Picture

Project no:

Name:_____

For:_____

Date started: _____ Date finished : _____

Pattern:_____

Fabric:_____

Color:_____

Purchased from:_____

Cost: _____

Fabric:_____

Color:_____

Purchased from:_____

Cost:_____

Fabric:_____

Color:_____

Purchased from:_____

Cost: _____

Progress Checklist:

☐ Fabric pulled   ☐ Backing made

☐ Fabric cut   ☐ Quilt basted

☐ Blocks made   ☐ Quilting done

☐ Rows sewn   ☐ Binding made

☐ Borders on   ☐ Binding on

Notes:_____

_____

_____

_____

_____

_____

Design

Picture

Project no:

Name:_____

For:_____

Date started: _____ Date finished : _____

Pattern: _____

Fabric:_____

Color:_____

Purchased from:_____

Cost:_____

Fabric:_____

Color:_____

Purchased from:_____

Cost:_____

Fabric:_____

Color:_____

Purchased from:_____

Cost:_____

Progress Checklist:

☐ Fabric pulled   ☐ Backing made

☐ Fabric cut   ☐ Quilt basted

☐ Blocks made   ☐ Quilting done

☐ Rows sewn   ☐ Binding made

☐ Borders on   ☐ Binding on

Notes:_____

_____

_____

_____

_____

_____

Design

Picture

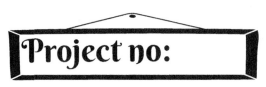

Project no:

Name:_____

For:_____

Date started: _____ Date finished : _____

Pattern: _____

Fabric:_____

Color:_____

Purchased from:_____

Cost:_____

Fabric:_____

Color:_____

Purchased from:_____

Cost:_____

Fabric:_____

Color:_____

Purchased from:_____

Cost:_____

Progress Checklist:

☐ Fabric pulled   ☐ Backing made

☐ Fabric cut   ☐ Quilt basted

☐ Blocks made   ☐ Quilting done

☐ Rows sewn   ☐ Binding made

☐ Borders on   ☐ Binding on

Notes:_____

_____

_____

_____

_____

_____

Design

Picture

Project no:

Name:_____

For:_____

Date started: _____ Date finished : _____

Pattern: _____

Fabric:_____

Color:_____

Purchased from:_____

Cost: _____

Fabric:_____

Color:_____

Purchased from:_____

Cost: _____

Fabric:_____

Color:_____

Purchased from:_____

Cost: _____

Progress Checklist:

☐ Fabric pulled   ☐ Backing made

☐ Fabric cut   ☐ Quilt basted

☐ Blocks made   ☐ Quilting done

☐ Rows sewn   ☐ Binding made

☐ Borders on   ☐ Binding on

Notes:_____

_____

_____

_____

_____

_____

Design

Picture

Project no:

Name:_____

For:_____

Date started: _____ Date finished : _____

Pattern: _____

Fabric:_____

Color:_____

Purchased from:_____

Cost: _____

Fabric:_____

Color:_____

Purchased from:_____

Cost: _____

Fabric:_____

Color:_____

Purchased from:_____

Cost: _____

Progress Checklist:

☐ Fabric pulled   ☐ Backing made

☐ Fabric cut   ☐ Quilt basted

☐ Blocks made   ☐ Quilting done

☐ Rows sewn   ☐ Binding made

☐ Borders on   ☐ Binding on

Notes:_____

_____

_____

_____

_____

_____

_____

Design

Picture

Project no:

Name:_____

For:_____

Date started: _____   Date finished : _____

Pattern: _____

Fabric:_____

Color:_____

Purchased from:_____

Cost:_____

Fabric:_____

Color:_____

Purchased from:_____

Cost:_____

Fabric:_____

Color:_____

Purchased from:_____

Cost:_____

Progress Checklist:

☐ Fabric pulled   ☐ Backing made

☐ Fabric cut   ☐ Quilt basted

☐ Blocks made   ☐ Quilting done

☐ Rows sewn   ☐ Binding made

☐ Borders on   ☐ Binding on

Notes:_____

_____

_____

_____

_____

_____

Design

Picture

Project no:

Name:_____

For:_____

Date started: _____ Date finished : _____

Pattern: _____

Fabric:_____
Color:_____
Purchased from:_____
Cost:_____

Fabric:_____
Color:_____
Purchased from:_____
Cost:_____

Fabric:_____
Color:_____
Purchased from:_____
Cost:_____

Progress Checklist:

☐ Fabric pulled   ☐ Backing made
☐ Fabric cut   ☐ Quilt basted
☐ Blocks made   ☐ Quilting done
☐ Rows sewn   ☐ Binding made
☐ Borders on   ☐ Binding on

Notes:_____
_____
_____
_____
_____
_____

Design

Picture

Project no:

Name:_____

For:_____

Date started: _____ Date finished : _____

Pattern:_____

Fabric:_____

Color:_____

Purchased from:_____

Cost: _____

Fabric:_____

Color:_____

Purchased from:_____

Cost: _____

Fabric:_____

Color:_____

Purchased from:_____

Cost: _____

Progress Checklist:

☐ Fabric pulled ☐ Backing made

☐ Fabric cut ☐ Quilt basted

☐ Blocks made ☐ Quilting done

☐ Rows sewn ☐ Binding made

☐ Borders on ☐ Binding on

Notes:_____

_____

_____

_____

_____

_____

Design

Picture

Project no:

Name:_____

For:_____

Date started: _____ Date finished : _____

Pattern: _____

Fabric:_____

Color:_____

Purchased from:_____

Cost: _____

Fabric:_____

Color:_____

Purchased from:_____

Cost: _____

Fabric:_____

Color:_____

Purchased from:_____

Cost: _____

Progress Checklist:

☐ Fabric pulled   ☐ Backing made

☐ Fabric cut   ☐ Quilt basted

☐ Blocks made   ☐ Quilting done

☐ Rows sewn   ☐ Binding made

☐ Borders on   ☐ Binding on

Notes:_____

_____

_____

_____

_____

_____

Design

Picture

Project no:

Name:_____

For:_____

Date started: _____ Date finished : _____

Pattern:_____

Fabric:_____

Color:_____

Purchased from:_____

Cost:_____

Fabric:_____

Color:_____

Purchased from:_____

Cost:_____

Fabric:_____

Color:_____

Purchased from:_____

Cost:_____

Progress Checklist:

☐ Fabric pulled   ☐ Backing made

☐ Fabric cut   ☐ Quilt basted

☐ Blocks made   ☐ Quilting done

☐ Rows sewn   ☐ Binding made

☐ Borders on   ☐ Binding on

Notes:_____

_____

_____

_____

_____

_____

Design

Picture

Project no:

Name:_____

For:_____

Date started: _____ Date finished : _____

Pattern:_____

Fabric:_____

Color:_____

Purchased from:_____

Cost:_____

Fabric:_____

Color:_____

Purchased from:_____

Cost:_____

Fabric:_____

Color:_____

Purchased from:_____

Cost:_____

Progress Checklist:

☐ Fabric pulled   ☐ Backing made

☐ Fabric cut   ☐ Quilt basted

☐ Blocks made   ☐ Quilting done

☐ Rows sewn   ☐ Binding made

☐ Borders on   ☐ Binding on

Notes:_____

_____

_____

_____

_____

_____

Design

Picture

Project no:

Name: _____

For: _____

Date started: _____ **Date finished :** _____

Pattern: _____

Fabric: _____

Color: _____

Purchased from: _____

Cost: _____

Fabric: _____

Color: _____

Purchased from: _____

Cost: _____

Fabric: _____

Color: _____

Purchased from: _____

Cost: _____

Progress Checklist:

☐ Fabric pulled ☐ Backing made

☐ Fabric cut ☐ Quilt basted

☐ Blocks made ☐ Quilting done

☐ Rows sewn ☐ Binding made

☐ Borders on ☐ Binding on

Notes: _____

_____

_____

_____

_____

_____

Design

Picture

Project no:

Name:_____

For:_____

Date started: _____ Date finished : _____

Pattern: _____

Fabric:_____
Color:_____
Purchased from:_____
Cost: _____

Fabric:_____
Color:_____
Purchased from:_____
Cost: _____

Fabric:_____
Color:_____
Purchased from:_____
Cost: _____

Progress Checklist:

☐ Fabric pulled   ☐ Backing made
☐ Fabric cut   ☐ Quilt basted
☐ Blocks made   ☐ Quilting done
☐ Rows sewn   ☐ Binding made
☐ Borders on   ☐ Binding on

Notes:_____
_____
_____
_____
_____
_____
_____

Design

Picture

Project no:

Name: _____

For: _____

Date started: _____ Date finished : _____

Pattern: _____

Fabric: _____

Color: _____

Purchased from: _____

Cost: _____

Fabric: _____

Color: _____

Purchased from: _____

Cost: _____

Fabric: _____

Color: _____

Purchased from: _____

Cost: _____

Progress Checklist:

☐ Fabric pulled   ☐ Backing made
☐ Fabric cut   ☐ Quilt basted
☐ Blocks made   ☐ Quilting done
☐ Rows sewn   ☐ Binding made
☐ Borders on   ☐ Binding on

Notes: _____
_____
_____
_____
_____
_____

Design

Picture

Project no:

Name:_____

For:_____

Date started: _____ Date finished : _____

Pattern: _____

Fabric:_____

Color:_____

Purchased from:_____

Cost: _____

Fabric:_____

Color:_____

Purchased from:_____

Cost: _____

Fabric:_____

Color:_____

Purchased from:_____

Cost: _____

Progress Checklist:

☐ Fabric pulled   ☐ Backing made

☐ Fabric cut   ☐ Quilt basted

☐ Blocks made   ☐ Quilting done

☐ Rows sewn   ☐ Binding made

☐ Borders on   ☐ Binding on

Notes:_____

_____

_____

_____

_____

_____

Design

Picture

Project no:

Name:_____

For:_____

Date started: _____ Date finished : _____

Pattern: _____

Fabric:_____

Color:_____

Purchased from:_____

Cost:_____

Fabric:_____

Color:_____

Purchased from:_____

Cost:_____

Fabric:_____

Color:_____

Purchased from:_____

Cost:_____

Progress Checklist:

☐ Fabric pulled   ☐ Backing made

☐ Fabric cut   ☐ Quilt basted

☐ Blocks made   ☐ Quilting done

☐ Rows sewn   ☐ Binding made

☐ Borders on   ☐ Binding on

Notes:_____

_____

_____

_____

_____

_____

Design

Picture

Project no:

Name:_____

For:_____

Date started: _____ Date finished : _____

Pattern: _____

Fabric:_____

Color:_____

Purchased from:_____

Cost:_____

Fabric:_____

Color:_____

Purchased from:_____

Cost:_____

Fabric:_____

Color:_____

Purchased from:_____

Cost:_____

Progress Checklist:

☐ Fabric pulled   ☐ Backing made

☐ Fabric cut   ☐ Quilt basted

☐ Blocks made   ☐ Quilting done

☐ Rows sewn   ☐ Binding made

☐ Borders on   ☐ Binding on

Notes:_____

_____

_____

_____

_____

_____

Design

Picture

Project no:

Name:_____

For:_____

Date started: _____ Date finished : _____

Pattern:_____

Fabric:_____

Color:_____

Purchased from:_____

Cost:_____

Fabric:_____

Color:_____

Purchased from:_____

Cost:_____

Fabric:_____

Color:_____

Purchased from:_____

Cost:_____

Progress Checklist:

☐ Fabric pulled   ☐ Backing made

☐ Fabric cut   ☐ Quilt basted

☐ Blocks made   ☐ Quilting done

☐ Rows sewn   ☐ Binding made

☐ Borders on   ☐ Binding on

Notes:_____

_____

_____

_____

_____

_____

Design

Picture

Project no:

Name: _____

For: _____

Date started: _____ **Date finished :** _____

Pattern: _____

Fabric: _____
Color: _____
Purchased from: _____
Cost: _____

Fabric: _____
Color: _____
Purchased from: _____
Cost: _____

Fabric: _____
Color: _____
Purchased from: _____
Cost: _____

Progress Checklist:

☐ Fabric pulled   ☐ Backing made
☐ Fabric cut   ☐ Quilt basted
☐ Blocks made   ☐ Quilting done
☐ Rows sewn   ☐ Binding made
☐ Borders on   ☐ Binding on

Notes: _____
_____
_____
_____
_____
_____

Design

Picture

Project no:

Name:_____

For:_____

Date started: _____ Date finished : _____

Pattern: _____

Fabric:_____
Color:_____
Purchased from:_____
Cost:_____

Fabric:_____
Color:_____
Purchased from:_____
Cost:_____

Fabric:_____
Color:_____
Purchased from:_____
Cost:_____

Progress Checklist:

☐ Fabric pulled   ☐ Backing made
☐ Fabric cut   ☐ Quilt basted
☐ Blocks made   ☐ Quilting done
☐ Rows sewn   ☐ Binding made
☐ Borders on   ☐ Binding on

Notes:_____
_____
_____
_____
_____
_____

Design

Picture

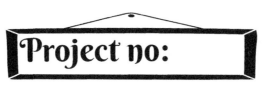

Project no:

Name:_____

For:_____

Date started: _____ Date finished : _____

Pattern: _____

Fabric:_____

Color:_____

Purchased from:_____

Cost: _____

Fabric:_____

Color:_____

Purchased from:_____

Cost: _____

Fabric:_____

Color:_____

Purchased from:_____

Cost: _____

Progress Checklist:

☐ Fabric pulled   ☐ Backing made

☐ Fabric cut   ☐ Quilt basted

☐ Blocks made   ☐ Quilting done

☐ Rows sewn   ☐ Binding made

☐ Borders on   ☐ Binding on

Notes:_____

_____

_____

_____

_____

_____

Design

Picture

Project no:

Name:_____

For:_____

Date started: _____ Date finished : _____

Pattern: _____

Fabric:_____
Color:_____
Purchased from:_____
Cost:_____

Fabric:_____
Color:_____
Purchased from:_____
Cost:_____

Fabric:_____
Color:_____
Purchased from:_____
Cost:_____

Progress Checklist:

☐ Fabric pulled   ☐ Backing made
☐ Fabric cut   ☐ Quilt basted
☐ Blocks made   ☐ Quilting done
☐ Rows sewn   ☐ Binding made
☐ Borders on   ☐ Binding on

Notes:_____
_____
_____
_____
_____
_____

Design

Picture

Project no:

Name:_____

For:_____

Date started: _____ Date finished : _____

Pattern: _____

Fabric:_____

Color:_____

Purchased from:_____

Cost: _____

Fabric:_____

Color:_____

Purchased from:_____

Cost: _____

Fabric:_____

Color:_____

Purchased from:_____

Cost: _____

Progress Checklist:

☐ Fabric pulled ☐ Backing made

☐ Fabric cut ☐ Quilt basted

☐ Blocks made ☐ Quilting done

☐ Rows sewn ☐ Binding made

☐ Borders on ☐ Binding on

Notes:_____

_____

_____

_____

_____

_____

Design

Picture

Project no:

Name:_____

For:_____

Date started: _____ Date finished : _____

Pattern: _____

Fabric:_____
Color:_____
Purchased from:_____
Cost:_____

Fabric:_____
Color:_____
Purchased from:_____
Cost:_____

Fabric:_____
Color:_____
Purchased from:_____
Cost:_____

Progress Checklist:

☐ Fabric pulled   ☐ Backing made
☐ Fabric cut   ☐ Quilt basted
☐ Blocks made   ☐ Quilting done
☐ Rows sewn   ☐ Binding made
☐ Borders on   ☐ Binding on

Notes:_____
_____
_____
_____
_____
_____

Design

Picture

Project no:

Name: _____

For: _____

Date started: _____ **Date finished :** _____

Pattern: _____

Fabric: _____

Color: _____

Purchased from: _____

Cost: _____

Fabric: _____

Color: _____

Purchased from: _____

Cost: _____

Fabric: _____

Color: _____

Purchased from: _____

Cost: _____

Progress Checklist:

☐ Fabric pulled   ☐ Backing made

☐ Fabric cut   ☐ Quilt basted

☐ Blocks made   ☐ Quilting done

☐ Rows sewn   ☐ Binding made

☐ Borders on   ☐ Binding on

Notes: _____

_____

_____

_____

_____

_____

Design

Picture

Project no:

Name:_____

For:_____

Date started: _____ Date finished : _____

Pattern: _____

Fabric:_____

Color:_____

Purchased from:_____

Cost:_____

Fabric:_____

Color:_____

Purchased from:_____

Cost:_____

Fabric:_____

Color:_____

Purchased from:_____

Cost:_____

Progress Checklist:

☐ Fabric pulled   ☐ Backing made

☐ Fabric cut   ☐ Quilt basted

☐ Blocks made   ☐ Quilting done

☐ Rows sewn   ☐ Binding made

☐ Borders on   ☐ Binding on

Notes:_____

_____

_____

_____

_____

_____

Design

Picture

Project no:

Name:_____

For:_____

Date started: _____ Date finished : _____

Pattern: _____

Fabric:_____

Color:_____

Purchased from:_____

Cost: _____

Fabric:_____

Color:_____

Purchased from:_____

Cost: _____

Fabric:_____

Color:_____

Purchased from:_____

Cost: _____

Progress Checklist:

☐ Fabric pulled   ☐ Backing made

☐ Fabric cut   ☐ Quilt basted

☐ Blocks made   ☐ Quilting done

☐ Rows sewn   ☐ Binding made

☐ Borders on   ☐ Binding on

Notes:_____

_____

_____

_____

_____

_____

Design

Picture

Project no:

Name:_____

For:_____

Date started: _____ Date finished : _____

Pattern: _____

Fabric:_____

Color:_____

Purchased from:_____

Cost:_____

Fabric:_____

Color:_____

Purchased from:_____

Cost:_____

Fabric:_____

Color:_____

Purchased from:_____

Cost:_____

Progress Checklist:

☐ Fabric pulled   ☐ Backing made

☐ Fabric cut   ☐ Quilt basted

☐ Blocks made   ☐ Quilting done

☐ Rows sewn   ☐ Binding made

☐ Borders on   ☐ Binding on

Notes:_____

_____

_____

_____

_____

_____

Design

Picture

Project no:

Name:_____

For:_____

Date started: _____ Date finished : _____

Pattern: _____

Fabric:_____

Color:_____

Purchased from:_____

Cost: _____

Fabric:_____

Color:_____

Purchased from:_____

Cost: _____

Fabric:_____

Color:_____

Purchased from:_____

Cost: _____

Progress Checklist:

☐ Fabric pulled ☐ Backing made

☐ Fabric cut ☐ Quilt basted

☐ Blocks made ☐ Quilting done

☐ Rows sewn ☐ Binding made

☐ Borders on ☐ Binding on

Notes:_____

_____

_____

_____

_____

_____

Design

Picture

Project no:

Name:_____

For:_____

Date started: _____ Date finished : _____

Pattern: _____

Fabric:_____
Color:_____
Purchased from:_____
Cost:_____

Fabric:_____
Color:_____
Purchased from: _____
Cost:_____

Fabric:_____
Color:_____
Purchased from:_____
Cost:_____

Progress Checklist:

☐ Fabric pulled   ☐ Backing made

☐ Fabric cut   ☐ Quilt basted

☐ Blocks made   ☐ Quilting done

☐ Rows sewn   ☐ Binding made

☐ Borders on   ☐ Binding on

Notes:_____

_____

_____

_____

_____

_____

Design

Picture

Project no:

Name:_____

For:_____

Date started: _____ Date finished : _____

Pattern: _____

Fabric:_____
Color:_____
Purchased from:_____
Cost: _____

Fabric:_____
Color:_____
Purchased from:_____
Cost: _____

Fabric:_____
Color:_____
Purchased from:_____
Cost: _____

Progress Checklist:

☐ Fabric pulled   ☐ Backing made
☐ Fabric cut   ☐ Quilt basted
☐ Blocks made   ☐ Quilting done
☐ Rows sewn   ☐ Binding made
☐ Borders on   ☐ Binding on

Notes:_____
_____
_____
_____
_____
_____

Design

Picture

Project no:

Name:_____

For:_____

Date started: _____ **Date finished :** _____

Pattern: _____

Fabric:_____

Color:_____

Purchased from:_____

Cost:_____

Fabric:_____

Color:_____

Purchased from:_____

Cost:_____

Fabric:_____

Color:_____

Purchased from:_____

Cost:_____

Progress Checklist:

☐ Fabric pulled   ☐ Backing made

☐ Fabric cut   ☐ Quilt basted

☐ Blocks made   ☐ Quilting done

☐ Rows sewn   ☐ Binding made

☐ Borders on   ☐ Binding on

Notes:_____

_____

_____

_____

_____

_____

Design

Picture

Project no:

Name:_____

For:_____

Date started: _____ Date finished : _____

Pattern: _____

Fabric:_____

Color:_____

Purchased from:_____

Cost: _____

Fabric:_____

Color:_____

Purchased from:_____

Cost: _____

Fabric:_____

Color:_____

Purchased from:_____

Cost: _____

Progress Checklist:

☐ Fabric pulled   ☐ Backing made

☐ Fabric cut   ☐ Quilt basted

☐ Blocks made   ☐ Quilting done

☐ Rows sewn   ☐ Binding made

☐ Borders on   ☐ Binding on

Notes:_____

_____

_____

_____

_____

_____

Design

Picture

Project no:

Name:_____

For:_____

Date started: _____ Date finished : _____

Pattern: _____

Fabric:_____
Color:_____
Purchased from:_____
Cost:_____

Fabric:_____
Color:_____
Purchased from:_____
Cost:_____

Fabric:_____
Color:_____
Purchased from:_____
Cost:_____

Progress Checklist:

☐ Fabric pulled   ☐ Backing made
☐ Fabric cut   ☐ Quilt basted
☐ Blocks made   ☐ Quilting done
☐ Rows sewn   ☐ Binding made
☐ Borders on   ☐ Binding on

Notes:_____

_____

_____

_____

_____

_____

Design

Picture

Project no:

Name:_____

For:_____

Date started: _____ **Date finished :** _____

Pattern: _____

Fabric:_____
Color:_____
Purchased from:_____
Cost: _____

Fabric:_____
Color:_____
Purchased from:_____
Cost: _____

Fabric:_____
Color:_____
Purchased from:_____
Cost: _____

Progress Checklist:

☐ Fabric pulled   ☐ Backing made

☐ Fabric cut   ☐ Quilt basted

☐ Blocks made   ☐ Quilting done

☐ Rows sewn   ☐ Binding made

☐ Borders on   ☐ Binding on

Notes:_____

_____

_____

_____

_____

_____

Design

Picture

Project no:

Name:_____

For:_____

Date started: _____ Date finished : _____

Pattern: _____

Fabric:_____
Color:_____
Purchased from:_____
Cost:_____

Fabric:_____
Color:_____
Purchased from:_____
Cost:_____

Fabric:_____
Color:_____
Purchased from:_____
Cost:_____

Progress Checklist:

☐ Fabric pulled   ☐ Backing made
☐ Fabric cut   ☐ Quilt basted
☐ Blocks made   ☐ Quilting done
☐ Rows sewn   ☐ Binding made
☐ Borders on   ☐ Binding on

Notes:_____
_____
_____
_____
_____
_____
_____

Design

Picture

Project no:

Name:_____

For:_____

Date started: _____ Date finished : _____

Pattern: _____

Fabric:_____

Color:_____

Purchased from:_____

Cost: _____

Fabric:_____

Color:_____

Purchased from:_____

Cost: _____

Fabric:_____

Color:_____

Purchased from:_____

Cost: _____

Progress Checklist:

☐ Fabric pulled   ☐ Backing made

☐ Fabric cut   ☐ Quilt basted

☐ Blocks made   ☐ Quilting done

☐ Rows sewn   ☐ Binding made

☐ Borders on   ☐ Binding on

Notes:_____

_____

_____

_____

_____

_____

Design

Picture

Project no:

Name: _____

For: _____

Date started: _____ **Date finished :** _____

Pattern: _____

Fabric: _____

Color: _____

Purchased from: _____

Cost: _____

Fabric: _____

Color: _____

Purchased from: _____

Cost: _____

Fabric: _____

Color: _____

Purchased from: _____

Cost: _____

Progress Checklist:

☐ Fabric pulled   ☐ Backing made

☐ Fabric cut   ☐ Quilt basted

☐ Blocks made   ☐ Quilting done

☐ Rows sewn   ☐ Binding made

☐ Borders on   ☐ Binding on

Notes: _____

_____

_____

_____

_____

_____

Design

Picture

Project no:

Name:_____

For:_____

Date started: _____ **Date finished :** _____

Pattern: _____

Fabric:_____

Color:_____

Purchased from:_____

Cost: _____

Fabric:_____

Color:_____

Purchased from: _____

Cost: _____

Fabric:_____

Color:_____

Purchased from:_____

Cost: _____

Progress Checklist:

☐ Fabric pulled ☐ Backing made

☐ Fabric cut ☐ Quilt basted

☐ Blocks made ☐ Quilting done

☐ Rows sewn ☐ Binding made

☐ Borders on ☐ Binding on

Notes:_____

_____

_____

_____

_____

_____

_____

Design

Picture

Project no:

Name:_____

For:_____

Date started: _____ Date finished : _____

Pattern: _____

Fabric:_____

Color:_____

Purchased from:_____

Cost:_____

Fabric:_____

Color:_____

Purchased from:_____

Cost:_____

Fabric:_____

Color:_____

Purchased from:_____

Cost:_____

Progress Checklist:

☐ Fabric pulled   ☐ Backing made

☐ Fabric cut   ☐ Quilt basted

☐ Blocks made   ☐ Quilting done

☐ Rows sewn   ☐ Binding made

☐ Borders on   ☐ Binding on

Notes:_____

_____

_____

_____

_____

_____

Design

Picture

Project no:

Name:_____

For:_____

Date started: _____ Date finished : _____

Pattern:_____

Fabric:_____

Color:_____

Purchased from:_____

Cost:_____

Fabric:_____

Color:_____

Purchased from:_____

Cost:_____

Fabric:_____

Color:_____

Purchased from:_____

Cost:_____

Progress Checklist:

☐ Fabric pulled   ☐ Backing made

☐ Fabric cut   ☐ Quilt basted

☐ Blocks made   ☐ Quilting done

☐ Rows sewn   ☐ Binding made

☐ Borders on   ☐ Binding on

Notes:_____

_____

_____

_____

_____

_____

Design

Picture

Project no:

Name:_____

For:_____

Date started: _____ Date finished : _____

Pattern: _____

Fabric:_____

Color:_____

Purchased from:_____

Cost: _____

Fabric:_____

Color:_____

Purchased from:_____

Cost: _____

Fabric:_____

Color:_____

Purchased from:_____

Cost: _____

Progress Checklist:

☐ Fabric pulled   ☐ Backing made

☐ Fabric cut   ☐ Quilt basted

☐ Blocks made   ☐ Quilting done

☐ Rows sewn   ☐ Binding made

☐ Borders on   ☐ Binding on

Notes:_____

_____

_____

_____

_____

_____

Design

Picture

Project no:

Name: _____

For: _____

Date started: _____ **Date finished :** _____

Pattern: _____

Fabric:_____

Color:_____

Purchased from:_____

Cost: _____

Fabric:_____

Color:_____

Purchased from:_____

Cost: _____

Fabric:_____

Color:_____

Purchased from:_____

Cost:_____

Progress Checklist:

☐ Fabric pulled ☐ Backing made

☐ Fabric cut ☐ Quilt basted

☐ Blocks made ☐ Quilting done

☐ Rows sewn ☐ Binding made

☐ Borders on ☐ Binding on

Notes:_____

_____

_____

_____

_____

Design

Picture

Project no:

Name:_____

For:_____

Date started: _____ Date finished : _____

Pattern: _____

Fabric:_____

Color:_____

Purchased from:_____

Cost:_____

Fabric:_____

Color:_____

Purchased from:_____

Cost:_____

Fabric:_____

Color:_____

Purchased from:_____

Cost:_____

Progress Checklist:

☐ Fabric pulled   ☐ Backing made

☐ Fabric cut   ☐ Quilt basted

☐ Blocks made   ☐ Quilting done

☐ Rows sewn   ☐ Binding made

☐ Borders on   ☐ Binding on

Notes:_____

_____

_____

_____

_____

_____

Design

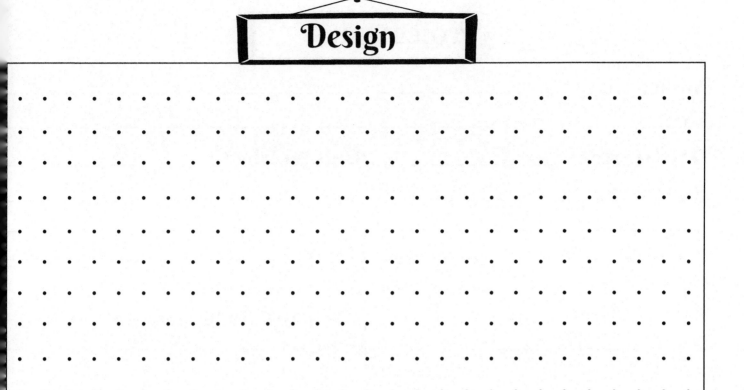

Picture

Project no:

Name: _____

For: _____

Date started: _____ **Date finished :** _____

Pattern: _____

Fabric: _____

Color: _____

Purchased from: _____

Cost: _____

Fabric: _____

Color: _____

Purchased from: _____

Cost: _____

Fabric: _____

Color: _____

Purchased from: _____

Cost: _____

Progress Checklist:

☐ Fabric pulled   ☐ Backing made

☐ Fabric cut   ☐ Quilt basted

☐ Blocks made   ☐ Quilting done

☐ Rows sewn   ☐ Binding made

☐ Borders on   ☐ Binding on

Notes: _____

_____

_____

_____

_____

_____

Design

Picture

Project no:

Name:_____

For:_____

Date started: _____ Date finished : _____

Pattern:_____

Fabric:_____

Color:_____

Purchased from:_____

Cost:_____

Fabric:_____

Color:_____

Purchased from:_____

Cost:_____

Fabric:_____

Color:_____

Purchased from:_____

Cost:_____

Progress Checklist:

☐ Fabric pulled   ☐ Backing made

☐ Fabric cut   ☐ Quilt basted

☐ Blocks made   ☐ Quilting done

☐ Rows sewn   ☐ Binding made

☐ Borders on   ☐ Binding on

Notes:_____

_____

_____

_____

_____

_____

Design

Picture

Project no:

Name:_____

For:_____

Date started: _____ **Date finished :** _____

Pattern: _____

Fabric:_____

Color:_____

Purchased from:_____

Cost: _____

Fabric:_____

Color:_____

Purchased from:_____

Cost: _____

Fabric:_____

Color:_____

Purchased from:_____

Cost: _____

Progress Checklist:

☐ Fabric pulled   ☐ Backing made

☐ Fabric cut   ☐ Quilt basted

☐ Blocks made   ☐ Quilting done

☐ Rows sewn   ☐ Binding made

☐ Borders on   ☐ Binding on

Notes:_____

_____

_____

_____

_____

_____

Design

Picture

Project no:

Name:_____

For:_____

Date started: _____ Date finished : _____

Pattern: _____

Fabric:_____
Color:_____
Purchased from:_____
Cost: _____

Fabric:_____
Color:_____
Purchased from: _____
Cost: _____

Fabric:_____
Color:_____
Purchased from:_____
Cost: _____

Progress Checklist:

☐ Fabric pulled   ☐ Backing made
☐ Fabric cut   ☐ Quilt basted
☐ Blocks made   ☐ Quilting done
☐ Rows sewn   ☐ Binding made
☐ Borders on   ☐ Binding on

Notes:_____
_____
_____
_____
_____
_____
_____

Design

Picture

Notes

Notes

Notes

Notes

Printed in Great Britain
by Amazon

33100422R00071